The Upanishads

Translation and Commentary by
Swami Paramananda
From the original Sanskrit text

RUPA

Published by
Rupa Publications India Pvt. Ltd 2023
161-B/4, Gulmohar House,
Yusuf Sarai Community Centre,
New Delhi 110049

Sales centres:
Bengaluru Chennai
Hyderabad Kolkata Mumbai

Copyright © Rupa Publications India Pvt. Ltd 2023

All rights reserved.
No part of this publication may be reproduced, transmitted,
or stored in a retrieval system, in any form or by any means,
electronic, mechanical, photocopying, recording or otherwise,
without the prior permission of the publisher.

P-ISBN: 978-93-5702-604-8
E-ISBN: 978-93-5702-606-2

Fourth impression 2025

10 9 8 7 6 5 4

Printed in India

This book is sold subject to the condition that it shall not,
by way of trade or otherwise, be lent, resold, hired out, or otherwise
circulated, without the publisher's prior consent, in any form of
binding or cover other than that in which it is published.

*This volume is reverently dedicated to all seekers
of truth and lovers of wisdom*

CONTENTS

Preface   *vii*
Introduction   *xi*

Isa-Upanishad   4

Katha-Upanishad   29
Part First   30
Part Second   50
Part Third   71
Part Fourth   86
Part Fifth   97
Part Sixth   106

Kena-Upanishad   124

Part First   125
Part Second   132
Part Third   139
Part Fourth   146

PREFACE

The translator's idea of rendering the Upanishads into clear simple English, accessible to Occidental readers, had its origin in a visit paid to a Boston friend in 1909. The gentleman, then battling with a fatal malady, took from his library shelf a translation of the Upanishads and, opening it, expressed deep regret that the obscure and unfamiliar form shut from him what he felt to be profound and vital teaching.

The desire to unlock the closed doors of this ancient treasure house, awakened at that time, led to a series of classes on the Upanishads at The Vedanta Centre of Boston during its early days in St. Botolph Street. The translation and commentary then given were transcribed and, after studious revision, were published in the Centre's monthly magazine, "The Message of the East," in 1913 and 1914.

Still further revision has brought it to its present form.

So far as was consistent with a faithful rendering of the Sanskrit text, the Swami throughout his translation has sought to eliminate all that might seem obscure and confusing to the modern mind. While retaining in remarkable measure the rhythm and archaic force of the lines, he has tried not to sacrifice directness and simplicity of style. Where he has been obliged to use the Sanskrit term for lack of an exact English equivalent, he has invariably interpreted it by a familiar English word in brackets; and everything has been done to remove the sense of strangeness in order that the Occidental reader may not feel himself an alien in the new regions of thought opened to him.

Even more has the Swami striven to keep the letter subordinate to the spirit. Any Scripture is only secondarily an historical document. To treat it as an object of mere intellectual curiosity is to cheat the world of

PREFACE

its deeper message. If mankind is to derive the highest benefit from a study of it, its appeal must be primarily to the spiritual consciousness; and one of the salient merits of the present translation lies in this, that the translator approaches his task not only with the grave concern of the careful scholar, but also with the profound reverence and fervor of the true devotee.

Editor

Boston, March, 1919

INTRODUCTION

The Upanishads represent the loftiest heights of ancient Indo-Aryan thought and culture. They form the wisdom portion or Gnana-Kanda of the Vedas, as contrasted with the Karma-Kanda or sacrificial portion. In each of the four great Vedas--known as Rik, Yajur, Sama and Atharva--there is a large portion which deals predominantly with rituals and ceremonials, and which has for its aim to show man how by the path of right action he may prepare himself for higher attainment. Following this in each Veda is another portion called the Upanishad, which deals wholly with the essentials of philosophic discrimination and ultimate spiritual vision. For this reason the Upanishads are known as the Vedanta, that is, the end or final goal of wisdom (Veda, wisdom; anta, end).

The name Upanishad has been variously interpreted. Many claim that it is a compound

Sanskrit word Upa-ni-shad, signifying "sitting at the feet or in the presence of a teacher"; while according to other authorities it means "to shatter" or "to destroy" the fetters of ignorance. Whatever may have been the technical reason for selecting this name, it was chosen undoubtedly to give a picture of aspiring seekers "approaching" some wise Seer in the seclusion of an Himalayan forest, in order to learn of him the profoundest truths regarding the cosmic universe and God. Because these teachings were usually given in the stillness of some distant retreat, where the noises of the world could not disturb the tranquillity of the contemplative life, they are known also as Aranyakas, Forest Books. Another reason for this name may be found in the fact that they were intended especially for the Vanaprasthas (those who, having fulfilled all their duties in the world, had retired to the forest to devote themselves to spiritual study).

The form which the teaching naturally assumed was that of dialogue, a form later

INTRODUCTION

adopted by Plato and other Greek philosophers. As nothing was written and all instruction was transmitted orally, the Upanishads are called Srutis, "what is heard." The term was also used in the sense of revealed, the Upanishads being regarded as direct revelations of God; while the Smritis, minor Scriptures "recorded through memory," were traditional works of purely human origin. It is a significant fact that nowhere in the Upanishads is mention made of any author or recorder.

No date for the origin of the Upanishads can be fixed, because the written text does not limit their antiquity. The word Sruti makes that clear to us. The teaching probably existed ages before it was set down in any written form. The text itself bears evidence of this, because not infrequently in a dialogue between teacher and disciple the teacher quotes from earlier Scriptures now unknown to us. As Professor Max Müller states in his lectures on the Vedanta Philosophy: "One feels certain that behind all these lightning-flashes of religious and philosophic thought there is a distant past, a dark background of which we shall never know the beginning." Some scholars place the Vedic period as far back as 4000 or 5000 B.C.; others from 2000 to 1400 B.C. But even the most conservative admit that it antedates, by several centuries at least, the Buddhistic period which begins in the sixth century B.C.

The value of the Upanishads, however, does not rest upon their antiquity, but upon the vital message they contain for all times and all peoples. There is nothing peculiarly racial or local in them. The ennobling lessons of these Scriptures are as practical for the modern world as they were for the Indo-Aryans of the earliest Vedic age. Their teachings are summed up in two Maha-Vakyam or "great sayings":--Tat twam asi (That thou art) and Aham Brahmasmi (I am Brahman). This oneness of Soul and God lies at the very root of all Vedic thought, and it is this dominant ideal of the unity of all life and the oneness of Truth which makes the study of the Upanishads especially beneficial at the present moment.

One of the most eminent of European Orientalists writes: "If we fix our attention upon it (this fundamental dogma of the Vedanta system) in its philosophical simplicity as the identity of God and the Soul, the Brahman and the Atman, it will be found to possess a significance reaching far beyond the Upanishads, their time and country; nay, we claim for it an inestimable value for the whole race of mankind.

Whatever new and unwonted paths the philosophy of the future may strike out, this principle will remain permanently unshaken and from it no deviation can possibly take place. If ever a general solution is reached of the great riddle . . . the key can only be found where alone the secret of nature lies open to us from within, that is to say, in our innermost self. It was here that for the first time the original thinkers of the Upanishads, to their immortal honor, found it...."

The first introduction of the Upanishads to the Western world was through a translation into Persian made in the seventeenth century. More than a century later the distinguished French scholar, Anquetil Duperron, brought a copy of the manuscript from Persia to France and translated it into French and Latin. Publishing only the Latin text. Despite the distortions which must have resulted from transmission through two alien languages, the light of the thought still shone with such brightness that it drew from Schopenhauer the fervent words: "How entirely does the Oupnekhat (Upanishad) breathe throughout the holy spirit of the Vedas! How is every one, who by a diligent study of its Persian Latin has become familiar with that incomparable book, stirred by that spirit to the very depth of his Soul! From every sentence deep, original and sublime thoughts arise, and the whole is pervaded by a high and holy and earnest spirit." Again he says: "The access to (the Vedas) by means of the Upanishads is in my eyes the greatest privilege which this still young century (1818) may claim before all previous centuries." This testimony is borne out by the thoughtful American scholar, Thoreau, who writes: "What extracts from the Vedas I have read fall on me like the light of a higher and purer luminary which describes a loftier course through a purer stratum free from particulars, simple, universal."

The first English translation was made by a learned Hindu, Raja Ram Mohun Roy (1775-1833). Since that time there have been various European translations--French, German, Italian and English. But a mere translation, however accurate and sympathetic, is not sufficient to make the Upanishads accessible to the Occidental mind. Professor Max Müller after a lifetime of arduous labor in this field frankly confesses: "Modern words are round, ancient words are square, and we may as well hope to solve the quadrature of the circle, as to express adequately the ancient thought of the Vedas in modern English."

Without a commentary it is practically impossible to understand either the spirit or the meaning of the Upanishads. They were never designed as popular Scriptures. They grew up essentially as text books of God-knowledge and Self-knowledge, and like all text books they need interpretation. Being transmitted orally from teacher to disciple, the style was necessarily extremely condensed and in the form of aphorisms. The language also was often metaphorical and obscure. Yet if one has the perseverance to penetrate beneath these mere surface difficulties, one is repaid a hundredfold; for these ancient Sacred Books contain the most precious gems of spiritual thought.

Every Upanishad begins with a Peace Chant (Shanti-patha) to create the proper atmosphere of purity and serenity. To study about God the whole nature must be prepared, so unitedly and with loving hearts teacher and disciples prayed to the Supreme Being for His grace and protection. It is not possible to comprehend the subtle problems of life unless the thought is tranquil and the energy concentrated. Until our mind is withdrawn from the varied distractions and agitations of worldly affairs, we cannot enter into the spirit of higher religious study. No study is of avail so long as our inner being is not attuned. We must hold a peaceful attitude towards all living things; and if it is lacking, we must strive fervently to cultivate it through suggestion by chanting or repeating some holy text. The same lesson is taught by Jesus the Christ when He says: "If thou bring thy gift to the altar and there rememberest that thy brother hath aught against thee; leave there thy gift before the altar and go thy way; first be reconciled to thy brother, and then come and offer thy gift."

Bearing this lofty ideal of peace in our minds, let us try to make our hearts free from prejudice, doubt and intolerance, so that from these sacred writings we may draw in abundance inspiration, love and wisdom.
Paramananda

ISA-UPANISHAD

This Upanishad desires its title from the opening words Isa-vasya, "God-covered." The use of Isa (Lord)—a more personal name of the Supreme Being than Brahman, Atman or Self, the names usually found in the Upanishads—constitutes one of its peculiarities. It forms the closing chapter of the Yajur-Veda, known as Shukla (White).

Oneness of the Soul and God, and the value of both faith and works as means of ultimate attainment are the leading themes of this Upanishad. The general teaching of the Upanishads is that works alone, even the highest, can bring only temporary happiness and must inevitably bind a man unless through them he gains knowledge of his real Self. To help him acquire this knowledge is the aim of this and all Upanishads.

ISA-UPANISHAD
Peace Chant

OM! That (the Invisible-Absolute) is whole; whole is this (the visible phenomenal); from the Invisible Whole comes forth the visible whole. Though the visible whole has come out from that Invisible Whole, yet the Whole remains unaltered.

OM! PEACE! PEACE! PEACE!

The indefinite term "That" is used in the Upanishads to designate the Invisible-Absolute, because no word or name can fully define It. A finite object, like a table or a tree, can be defined; but God, who is infinite and unbounded, cannot be expressed by finite language. Therefore the Rishis or Divine Seers, desirous not to limit the Unlimited, chose the indefinite term "That" to designate the Absolute.

ISA-UPANISHAD

In the light of true wisdom the phenomenal and the Absolute are inseparable. All existence is in the Absolute; and whatever exists, must exist in It; hence all manifestation is merely a modification of the One Supreme Whole, and neither increases nor diminishes It. The Whole therefore remains unaltered.

I

All this, whatsoever exists in the universe, should be covered by the Lord. Having renounced (the unreal), enjoy (the Real). Do not covet the wealth of any man.

We cover all things with the Lord by perceiving the Divine Presence everywhere. When the consciousness is firmly fixed in God, the conception of diversity naturally drops away; because the One Cosmic Existence shines through all things. As we gain the light of wisdom, we cease to cling to the unrealities of this world and we find all our joy in the realm of Reality.

The word "enjoy" is also interpreted by the great commentator Sankaracharya as "protect," because knowledge of our true Self is the greatest protector and sustainer. If we do not have this knowledge, we cannot be happy; because nothing on this external plane of phenomena is permanent or dependable. He who is rich in the knowledge of the Self does not covet external power or possession.

II

If one should desire to live in this world a hundred years, one should live performing Karma (righteous deeds). Thus thou mayest live; there is no other way. By doing this, Karma (the fruits of thy actions) will not defile thee.

If a man still clings to long life and earthly possessions, and is therefore unable to follow the path of Self-knowledge (Gnana-Nishta) as prescribed in the first Mantram (text), then he may follow the path of right action (Karma-Nishta). Karma here means actions performed without selfish motive, for the sake of the Lord alone. When a man performs actions clinging blindly to his lower desires, then his actions bind him to the plane of ignorance or the plane of birth and death; but when the same actions are performed with surrender to God, they purify and liberate him.

III

After leaving their bodies, they who have killed the Self go to the worlds of the Asuras, covered with blinding ignorance.

The idea of rising to bright regions as a reward for well-doers, and of falling into realms of darkness as a punishment for evil-doers is common to all great religions. But Vedanta claims that this condition of heaven and hell is only temporary; because our actions, being finite, can produce only a finite result.

What does it mean "to kill the Self?" How can the immortal Soul ever be destroyed? It cannot be destroyed, it can only be obscured. Those who hold themselves under the sway of ignorance, who serve the flesh and neglect the Atman or the real Self, are not able to perceive the effulgent and indestructible nature of their Soul; hence they fall into the realm where the Soul light does not shine. Here the Upanishad shows that the only hell is absence of knowledge. As long as man is overpowered by the darkness of ignorance, he is the slave of Nature and must accept whatever comes as the fruit of his thoughts and deeds. When he strays into the path of unreality, the Sages declare that he destroys himself; because he who clings to the perishable body and regards it as his true Self must experience death many times.

∽ IV ∽

That One, though motionless, is swifter than the mind. The senses can never overtake It, for It ever goes before. Though immovable, It travels faster than those who run. By It the all-pervading air sustains all living beings.

This verse explains the character of the Atman or Self. A finite object can be taken from one place and put in another, but it can only occupy one space at a time. The Atman, however, is present everywhere; hence, though one may run with the greatest swiftness to overtake It, already It is there before him.

Even the all-pervading air must be supported by this Self, since It is infinite; and as nothing can live without breathing air, all living things must draw their life from the Cosmic Self.

V

It moves and It moves not. It is far and also It is near. It is within and also It is without all this.

It is near to those who have the power to understand It, for It dwells in the heart of every one; but It seems far to those whose mind is covered by the clouds of sensuality and self-delusion. It is within, because It is the innermost Soul of all creatures; and It is without as the essence of the whole external universe, infilling it like the all-pervading ether.

∽ VI ∽

He who sees all beings in the Self and the Self in all beings, he never turns away from It (the Self).

∽ VII ∽

He who perceives all beings as the Self' for him how can there be delusion or grief, when he sees this oneness (everywhere) ?

He who perceives the Self everywhere never shrinks from anything, because through his higher consciousness he feels united with all life. When a man sees God in all beings and all beings in God, and also God dwelling in his own Soul, how can he hate any living thing? Grief and delusion rest upon a belief in diversity, which leads to competition and all forms of selfishness. With the realization of oneness, the sense of diversity vanishes and the cause of misery is removed.

~ VIII ~

He (the Self) is all-encircling, resplendent, bodiless, spotless, without sinews, pure, untouched by sin, all-seeing, all-knowing, transcendent, self-existent; He has disposed all things duly for eternal years.

ISA-UPANISHAD

This text defines the real nature of the Self. When our mind is cleansed from the dross of matter, then alone can we behold the vast, radiant, subtle, ever-pure and spotless Self, the true basis of our existence.

～ IX ～

They enter into blind darkness who worship Avidya (ignorance and delusion); they fall, as it were, into greater darkness who worship Vidya (knowledge).

X

By Vidya one end is attained; by Avidya, another. Thus we have heard from the wise men who taught this.

XI

He who knows at the same time both Vidya and Avidya, crosses over death by Avidya and attains immortality through Vidya.

Those who follow or "worship" the path of selfishness and pleasure (Avidya), without knowing anything higher, necessarily fall into darkness; but those who worship or cherish Vidya (knowledge) for mere intellectual pride and satisfaction, fall into greater darkness, because the opportunity which they misuse is greater.

In the subsequent verses Vidya and Avidya are used in something the same sense as "faith" and "works" in the Christian Bible; neither alone can lead to the ultimate goal, but when taken together they carry one to the Highest. Work done with unselfish motive purifies the mind and enables man to perceive his undying nature. From this he gains inevitably a knowledge of God, because the Soul and God are one and inseparable; and when he knows himself to be one with the Supreme and Indestructible Whole, he realizes his immortality.

∽ XII ∽

They fall into blind darkness who worship the Unmanifested and they fall into greater darkness who worship the manifested.

~ XIII ~

By the worship of the Unmanifested one end is attained; by the worship of the manifested, another. Thus we have heard from the wise men who taught us this.

~ XIV ~

He who knows at the same time both the Unmanifested (the cause of manifestation) and the destructible or manifested, he crosses over death through knowledge of the destructible and attains immortality through knowledge of the First Cause (Unmanifested).

This particular Upanishad deals chiefly with the Invisible Cause and the visible manifestation, and the whole trend of its teaching is to show that they are one and the same, one being the outcome of the other hence no perfect knowledge is possible without simultaneous comprehension of both. The wise men declare that he who worships in a one-sided way, whether the visible or the invisible, does not reach the highest goal. Only he who has a co-ordinated understanding of both the visible and the invisible, of matter and spirit, of activity and that which is behind activity, conquers Nature and thus overcomes death. By work, by making the mind steady and by following the prescribed rules given in the Scriptures, a man gains wisdom. By the light of that wisdom he is able to perceive the Invisible Cause in all visible forms. Therefore the wise man sees Him in every manifested form. They who have a true conception of God are never separated from Him. They exist in Him and He in them.

XV

The face of Truth is hidden by a golden disk. O Pushan (Effulgent Being)! Uncover (Thy face) that I, the worshipper of Truth, may behold Thee.

XVI

O Pushan! O Sun, sole traveller of the heavens, controller of all, son of Prajapati, withdraw Thy rays and gather up Thy burning effulgence. Now through Thy Grace I behold Thy blessed and glorious form. The Purusha (Effulgent Being) who dwells within Thee, I am He.

Here the sun, who is the giver of all light, is used as the symbol of the Infinite, giver of all wisdom. The seeker after Truth prays to the Effulgent One to control His dazzling rays, that his eyes, no longer blinded by them, may behold the Truth. Having perceived It, he proclaims: "Now I see that that Effulgent Being and I are one and the same, and my delusion is destroyed." By the light of Truth he is able to discriminate between the real and the unreal, and the knowledge thus gained convinces him that he is one with the Supreme; that there is no difference between himself and the Supreme Truth; or as Christ said, "I and my Father are one."

~ XVII ~

May my life-breath go to the all-pervading and immortal Prana, and let this body be burned to ashes. Om! O mind, remember thy deeds! O mind, remember, remember thy deeds! Remember!

Seek not fleeting results as the reward

of thy actions, O mind! Strive only for the Imperishable. This Mantram or text is often chanted at the hour of death to remind one of the perishable nature of the body and the eternal nature of the Soul. When the clear vision of the distinction between the mortal body and the immortal Soul dawns in the heart, then all craving for physical pleasure or material possession drops away; and one can say, let the body be burned to ashes that the Soul may attain its freedom; for death is nothing more than the casting-off of a worn-out garment.

ISA-UPANISHAD

～ XVIII ～

O Agni (Bright Being)! Lead us to blessedness by the good path. O Lord! Thou knowest all our deeds, remove all evil and delusion from us. To Thee we offer our prostrations and supplications again and again.

HERE ENDS THIS UPANISHAD

This Upanishad is called Isa-Vasya-Upanishad, that which gives Brahma-Vidya or knowledge of the All-pervading Deity. The dominant thought running through it is that we cannot enjoy life or realize true happiness unless we consciously "cover" all with the Omnipresent Lord. If we are not fully conscious of that which sustains our life, how can we live wisely and perform our duties? Whatever we see, movable or immovable, good or bad, it is all "That." We must not divide our conception of the universe; for in dividing it, we have only fragmentary knowledge and we thus limit ourselves.

He who sees all beings in his Self and his Self in all beings, he never suffers; because when he sees all creatures within his true Self, then jealousy, grief and hatred vanish. He alone can love. That AH-pervading One is self- effulgent, birthless, deathless, pure, untainted by sin and sorrow. Knowing this, he becomes free from the bondage of matter and transcends death. Transcending death means realizing the difference between body and Soul and identifying oneself with the Soul. When we actually behold the undecaying Soul within us and realize our true nature, we no longer identify ourself with the body which dies and we do not die with the body.

Self-knowledge has always been the theme of the Sages; and the Upanishads deal especially with the knowledge of the Self and also with the knowledge of God, because there is no difference between the Self and God. They are one and the same. That which comes out of the Infinite Whole must also be infinite; hence the Self is infinite. That is the ocean, we are the drops. So long as the drop remains separate from the ocean, it is small and weak; but when it is one with the ocean, then it has all the strength of the ocean. Similarly, so long as man believes himself to be separate from the Whole, he is helpless; but when he identifies himself with It, then he transcends all weakness and partakes of Its omnipotent qualities.

KATHA-UPANISHAD

KATHA-UPANISHAD

The Katha-Upanishad is probably the most widely known of all the Upanishads. It was early translated into Persian and through this rendering first made its way into Europe. Later Raja Ram Mohun Roy brought out an English version. It has since appeared in various languages; and English, German and French writers are all agreed in pronouncing it one of the most perfect expressions of the religion and philosophy of the Vedas. Sir Edwin Arnold popularized it by his metrical rendering under the name of "The Secret of Death," and Ralph Waldo Emerson gives its story in brief at the close of his essay on "Immortality."

There is no consensus of opinion regarding the place of this Upanishad in Vedic literature. Some authorities declare it to belong to the Yajur-Veda, others to the Sama-Veda, while a large number put it down as a part of the Atharva-Veda. The story is first suggested in the Rig-Veda; it is told more definitely in the Yajur-Veda; and in the Katha-Upanishad it appears fully elaborated and interwoven with the loftiest

Vedic teaching. There is nothing however, to indicate the special place of this final version, nor has any meaning been found for the name Katha.

The text presents a dialogue between an aspiring disciple, Nachiketas, and the Ruler of Death regarding the great Hereafter.

KATHA-UPANISHAD

Peace Chant

May He (the Supreme Being) protect us both, teacher and taught. May He be pleased with us. May we acquire strength. May our study bring us illumination. May there be no enmity among us.

OM! PEACE! PEACE! PEACE!

THE UPANISHADS

PART FIRST

∾ I ∾

Vahasrava, being desirous of heavenly rewards (at the Viswajit sacrifice), made a gift of all that he possessed. He had a son by the name of Nachiketas.

∾ II ∾

When the offerings were being distributed, faith (Shraddha) entered (the heart of) Nachiketas, who, though young, yet resected:

III

These cows have drunk water, eaten grass and given milk for the last time, and their senses have lost all vigour. He who gives these undoubtedly goes to joyless realms.

In India the idea of sacrifice has always been to give freely for the joy of giving, without asking anything in return; and the whole purpose and merit of the sacrifice is lost, if the giver entertains the least thought of name, fame or individual benefit. The special Viswajit sacrifice which Vajasrava was making required of him to give away all that he possessed. When, however, the gifts were brought forward to be offered, his son Nachiketas, although probably a lad about twelve years of age, observed how worthless were the animals which his father was offering. His heart at once became filled with Shraddha. There is no one English word which can convey the meaning of this

Sanskrit term. It is more than mere faith. It also implies self-reliance, an independent sense of right and wrong, and the courage of one's own conviction. As a boy of tender age, Nachiketas had no right to question his father's action; yet, impelled by the sudden awakening of his higher nature, he could not but reflect: "By merely giving these useless cows, my father cannot gain any merit. If he has vowed to give all his possessions, then he must also give me. Otherwise his sacrifice will not be complete and fruitful." Therefore, anxious for his father's welfare, he approached him gently and reverently.

KATHA-UPANISHAD

IV

He said to his father: Dear father, to whom wilt thou give me? He said it a second time, then a third time. The father replied: I shall give thee unto Death.

Nachiketas, being a dutiful son and eager to atone for his father's inadequate sacrifice, tried to remind him thus indirectly that he had not fulfilled his promise to give away all his possessions, since he had not yet offered his own son, who would be a worthier gift than useless cattle. His father, conscious that he was not making a true sacrifice, tried to ignore the boy's questions; but irritated by his persistence, he at last impatiently made answer: "I give thee to Yama, the Lord of Death." The fact that anger could so quickly rise in his heart proved that he had not the proper attitude of a sacrificer, who must always be tranquil, uplifted and free from egoism.

V

Nachiketas thought: Among many (of my father's pupils) I stand first; among many (others) I stand in the middle (but never last). What will be accomplished for my father by my going this day to Yama?

It was not conceit which led Nachiketas to consider his own standing and importance. He was weighing his value as a son and pupil in order to be able to judge whether or not he had merit enough to prove a worthy gift. Although he realized that his father's harsh reply was only the expression of a momentary outburst of anger; yet he believed that greater harm might befall his father, if his word was not kept. Therefore he sought to strengthen his father's resolution by reminding him of the transitory condition of life. He said:

VI

Look back to those who lived before and look to those who live now. Like grain the mortal decays and like grain again springs up (is reborn).

All things perish, Truth alone remains. Why then fear to sacrifice me also; Thus Nachiketas convinced his father that he should remain true to his word and send him to Yama, the Ruler of Death. Then Nachiketas went to the abode of Death, but Yama was absent and the boy waited without food or drink for three days. On Yama's return one of his household said to him:

VII

Like fire a Brahmana guest enters into houses. That fire is quenched by an offering. (Therefore) O Vaivaswata, bring water.

VIII

The foolish man in whose house a Brahmana guest remains without food, all his hopes and expectations, all the merit gained by his association with the holy, by his good words and deeds, all his sons and cattle, are destroyed.

According to the ancient Vedic ideal a guest is the representative of God and should be received with due reverence and honor. Especially is this the case with a Brahmana or a Sannyasin whose life is wholly consecrated to God. Any one who fails to give proper care to a holy guest brings misfortune on himself and his household. When Yama returned, therefore, one of the members of his household anxiously informed him of Nachiketas' presence and begged him to bring water to wash his feet, this being always the first service to an arriving guest.

~ IX ~

Yama said: O Brahmana! Revered guest! My salutations to thee. As thou hast remained three nights in my house without food, therefore choose three boons, O Brahmana.

X

Nachiketas said: May Gautama, my father, be free from anxious thought (about me). May he lose all anger (towards me) and be pacified in heart. May he know and welcome me when I am sent back by thee. This, O Death, is the first of the three boons I choose.

XI

Yama replied: Through my will Auddalaki Aruni (thy father) will know thee, and be again towards thee as before. He will sleep in peace at night. He will be free from wrath when he sees thee released from the mouth of death.

KATHA-UPANISHAD

∾ XII ∾

Nachiketas said: In the realm of heaven there is no fear, thou (Death) art not there; nor is there fear of old age. Having crossed beyond both hunger and thirst and being above grief, (they) rejoice in heaven.

∾ XIII ∾

Thou knowest, O Death, the fire-sacrifice that leads to heaven. Tell this to me, who am full of Shraddha (faith and yearning). They who live in the realm of heaven enjoy freedom from death. This I beg as my second boon.

~ XIV ~

Yama replied: I know well that fire which leads to the realm of heaven. I shall tell it to thee. Listen to me. Know, O Nachiketas, that this is the means of attaining endless worlds and their support. It is hidden in the heart of all beings.

~ XV ~

Yama then told him that fire-sacrifice, the beginning of all the worlds; what bricks, how many and how laid for the altar. Nachiketas repeated all as it was told to him. Then Death, being pleased with him, again said:

KATHA-UPANISHAD

～ XVI ～

The great-soured Yama, being well pleased, said to him (Nachiketas): I give thee now another boon. This fire (sacrifice) shall be named after thee. Take also this garland of many colours.

～ XVII ～

He who performs this Nachiketa fire-sacrifice three times, being united with the three (mother, father and teacher), and who fulfills the three-fold duty (study of the Vedas, sacrifice and alms-giving) crosses over birth and death. Knowing this worshipful shining fire, born of Brahman, and realizing Him, he attains eternal peace.

∽ XVIII ∽

He who knows the three-fold Nachiketa fire and performs the Nachiketa fire-sacrifice with three-fold knowledge, having cast off the fetters of death and being beyond grief, he rejoices in the realm of heaven.

∽ XIX ∽

O Nachiketas, this is thy fire that leads to heaven, which thou hast chosen as thy second boon. People will call this fire after thy name. Ask the third boon, Nachiketas.

Fire is regarded as "the foundation of all the worlds," because it is the revealer of creation. If there were no fire or light, no manifested form would be visible. We read in the Semitic Scriptures, "In the beginning the Lord said, 'Let there be light.'" Therefore, that which stands in the external universe as one of the purest symbols of the Divine, also dwells in subtle form in the heart of every living being as the vital energy, the life-force or cause of existence.

Yama now tells Nachiketas how, by performing sacrifice with the three-fold knowledge, he may transcend grief and death and reach heaven. The three-fold knowledge referred to is regarding the preparation of the altar and fire. Nachiketas being eager to learn, listened with wholehearted attention and was able to repeat all that was told him. This so pleased Yama that he granted him the extra boon of naming the fire-sacrifice after him and gave him a garland set with precious stones.

Verses XVI-XVIII are regarded by many as an interpolation, which would account for certain obscurities and repetitions in them.

XX

Nachiketas said: There is this doubt regarding what becomes of a man after death. Some say he exists, others that he does not exist. This knowledge I desire, being instructed by thee. Of the boons this is the third boon.

XXI

Yama replied: Even the Devas (Bright Ones) of old doubted regarding this. It is not easy to know; subtle indeed is this subject. O Nachiketas, choose another boon. Do not press me. Ask not this boon of me.

KATHA-UPANISHAD

∽ XXII ∽

Nachiketas said: O Death, thou sayest that even the Devas had doubts about this, and that it is not easy to know. Another teacher like unto thee is not to be found. Therefore no other boon can be equal to this one.

∽ XXIII ∽

Yama said: Ask for sons and grandsons who shall live a hundred years, many cattle, elephants, gold and horses. Ask for lands of vast extent and live thyself as many autumns as thou desirest.

~ XXIV ~

If thou thinkest of any other boon equal to this, ask for wealth and long life; be ruler over the wide earth. O Nachiketas, I shall make thee enjoyer of all desires.

~ XXV ~

Whatsoever objects of desire are difficult to obtain in the realm of mortals, ask them all as thou desirest; these lovely maidens with their chariots and musical instruments, such as are not obtainable by mortals—be served by these whom I give to thee. O Nachiketas, do not ask regarding death.

The third boon asked by Nachiketas concerning the great Hereafter was one which could be granted only to those who were freed from all mortal desires and limitations, therefore Yama first tested Nachiketas to see whether he was ready to receive such knowledge. "Do not press me regarding this secret," he said. "Even wise men cannot understand it and thou art a mere lad. Take, rather, long life, wealth, whatever will give thee happiness on the mortal plane." But the boy proved his strength and worthiness by remaining firm in his resolution to know the great secret of life and death.

~ XXVI ~

Nachiketas said: O Death, these are fleeting; they weaken the vigour of all the senses in man. Even the longest life is short. Keep thou thy chariots, dance and music.

XXVII

Man cannot be satisfied by wealth. Shall we possess wealth when we see thee (Death)? Shall we continue to live as long as thou rulest? Therefore that boon alone is to be chosen by me.

XXVIII

What man dwelling on the decaying mortal plane, having approached the undecaying immortal one, and having reflected upon the nature of enjoyment through beauty and sense pleasure, would delight in long life?

XXIX

O Death, that regarding which there is doubt, of the great Hereafter, tell us. Nachiketas asks for no other boon than that which penetrates this hidden secret.

PART SECOND

~ I ~

Yama said: The good is one thing and the pleasant another. These two, having different ends, bind a man. It is well with him who chooses the good. He who chooses the pleasant misses the true end.

~ II ~

The good and the pleasant approach man; the wise examines both and discriminates between them; the wise prefers the good to the pleasant, but the foolish man chooses the pleasant through love of bodily pleasure.

KATHA-UPANISHAD

~ III ~

O Nachiketas after wise reflection thou hast renounced the pleasant and all pleasing forms. Thou hast not accepted this garland of great value for which many mortals perish.

~ IV ~

Wide apart are these two,—ignorance and what is known as wisdom, leading in opposite directions. I believe Nachiketas to be one who longs for wisdom, since many tempting objects have not turned thee aside.

With this second part, the Ruler of Death begins his instructions regarding the great Hereafter. There are two paths,—one leading Godward, the other leading to worldly pleasure. He who follows one inevitably goes away from the other; because, like light and darkness they conflict. One leads to the imperishable spiritual realm; the other to the perishable physical realm. Both confront a man at every step of life. The discerning man distinguishing between the two, chooses the Real and Eternal, and he alone attains the highest, while the ignorant man, preferring that which brings him immediate and tangible results, misses the true purpose of his existence. Although Yama put before Nachiketas many temptations to test his sincerity and earnestness, he judging them at their real value, refused them all, saying "I have come from the mortal realm, shall I ask for what is mortal? I desire only that which is eternal." Then Death said to him: "I now see that thou art a sincere desirer of Truth. I offered thee vast wealth, long life and every form of pleasure which tempts and deludes men; but thou hast proved thy worthiness by rejecting them all."

V

Fools dwelling in ignorance, yet imagining themselves wise and learned, go round and round in crooked ways, like the blind led by the blind.

VI

The Hereafter never rises before the thoughtless child (the ignorant), deluded by the glamour of wealth. "This world alone is, there is none other": thinking thus, he falls under my sway again and again.

There are many in the world, who, puffed up with intellectual conceit, believe that they are capable of guiding others. But although they may possess a certain amount of worldly wisdom, they are devoid of deeper understanding; therefore all that they say merely increases doubt and confusion in the minds of those who hear them. Hence they are likened to blind men leading the blind.

The Hereafter does not shine before those who are lacking in the power of discrimination and are easily carried away therefore by the charm of fleeting objects. As children are tempted by toys, so they are tempted by pleasure, power, name and fame. To them these seem the only realities. Being thus attached to perishable things, they come many times under the dominion of death. There is one part of us which must die; there is another part which never dies. When a man can identify himself with his undying nature, which is one with God, then he overcomes death.

VII

He about whom many are not even able to hear, whom many cannot comprehend even after hearing: wonderful is the teacher, wonderful is he who can receive when taught by an able teacher.

Throughout the Vedic Scriptures it is declared that no one can impart spiritual knowledge unless he has realization. What is meant by realization? It means knowledge based on direct perception. In India often the best teachers have no learning, but their character is so shining that every one learns merely by coming in contact with them. In one of the Scriptures we read: Under a banyan tree sat a youthful teacher and beside him an aged disciple. The mind of the disciple was full of doubts and questions, but although the teacher continued silent, gradually every doubt vanished from the disciple's mind. This signifies that the conveying of spiritual teaching does not depend upon words only. It is the life, the illumination, which counts. Such God-enlightened men, however, cannot easily be found; but even with such a teacher, the knowledge of the Self cannot be gained unless the heart of the disciple is open and ready for the Truth. Hence Yama says both teacher and taught must be wonderful.

~ VIII ~

When taught by a man of inferior understanding, this Atman cannot be truly known, even though frequently thought upon. There is no way (to know It) unless it is taught by another (an illumined teacher), for it is subtler than the subtle and beyond argument.

KATHA-UPANISHAD

~ IX ~

O Dearest, this Atman cannot be attained by argument; It is truly known only when taught by another (a wise teacher). O Nachiketas, thou hast attained It. Thou art fixed in Truth. May we ever, find a questioner like thee.

Knowledge of the Atman or Self cannot be attained when it is taught by those who themselves lack in real understanding of It; and who therefore, having no definite conviction of their own, differ among themselves as to its nature and existence. Only he who has been able to perceive the Self directly, through the unfoldment of his higher nature, can proclaim what It actually is; and his words alone carry weight and bring illumination. It is too subtle to be reached by argument. This secret regarding the Hereafter cannot be known through reasoning or mere intellectual gymnastics. It is to be attained only in a state of consciousness which transcends the boundary line of reason.

～ X ～

I know that (earthly) treasure is transitory, for the eternal can never be attained by things which are non-eternal. Hence the Nachiketa fire (sacrifice) has been performed by me with perishable things and yet I have attained the eternal.

～ XI ～

O Nachiketas, thou hast seen the fulfillment of all desires, the basis of the universe, the endless fruit of sacrificial rites, the other shore where there is no fear, that which is praiseworthy, the great and wide support; yet, being wise, thou hast rejected all with firm resolve.

The teacher, saying that the imperishable cannot be attained by the perishable, shows that no amount of observance of rituals and ceremonies can earn the imperishable and eternal. Although the Nachiketa fire-sacrifice may bring results which seem eternal to mortals because of their long duration, yet they too must come to an end; therefore this sacrifice cannot lead to the final goal. Yama praises Nachiketas because, when all heavenly and earthly pleasures, as well as knowledge of all realms and their enjoyments were offered him, yet he cast them aside and remained firm in his desire for Truth alone.

∾ XII ∾

The wise, who by means of the highest meditation on the Self knows the Ancient One, difficult to perceive, seated in the innermost recess, hidden in the cave of the heart, dwelling in the depth of inner being, (he who knows that One) as God, is liberated from the fetters of joy and sorrow.

~ XIII ~

A mortal, having heard and fully grasped this, and having realized through discrimination the subtle Self, rejoices, because he has obtained that which is the source of all joy. I think the abode (of Truth) is open to Nachiketas.

The Scriptures give three stages in all spiritual attainment. The aspirant must first hear about the Truth from an enlightened teacher; next he must reflect upon what he has heard; then by constant practice of discrimination and meditation he realizes it; and with realization comes the fulfilment of every desire, because it unites him with the source of all. Having beheld this, a man learns that all sense pleasures are but fragmentary reflections of that one supreme joy, which can be found in the true Self alone. Yama assures Nachiketas that there is no doubt of his realizing the Truth, because he has shown the highest discrimination as well as fixity of purpose.

∽ XIV ∽

Nachiketas said: That which thou seest, which is neither virtue nor vice, neither cause nor effect, neither past nor future (but beyond these), tell me That.

XV

Yama replied: That goal which all the Vedas glorify, which all austerities proclaim, desiring which (people) practice Brahmacharya (a life of continence and service), that goal I tell thee briefly—it is Aum.

What name can man give to God? How can the Infinite be bound by any finite word? All that language can express must be finite, since it is itself finite. Yet it is very difficult for mortals to think or speak of anything without calling it by a definite name. Knowing this, the Sages gave to the Supreme the name A-U-M which stands as the root of all language. The first letter "A" is the mother-sound, being the natural sound uttered by every creature when the throat is opened, and no sound can be made without opening the throat. The last letter "M," spoken by closing the lips, terminates all articulation. As one carries the sound from the throat to the lips, it passes through the sound "U." These three sounds therefore cover the whole field of possible articulate sound. Their combination is called the Akshara or the imperishable word, the Sound-Brahman or the Word God, because it is the most universal name which can be given to the Supreme. Hence it must be the word which was "in the beginning" and corresponds to the Logos of Christian theology. It is because of the all-embracing significance of this name that it is used so universally in the Vedic Scriptures to designate the Absolute.

～ XVI ～

This Word is indeed Brahman. This Word is indeed the Supreme. He who knows this Word obtains whatever he desires.

~ XVII ~

This is the best Support, This is the highest Support; he who knows this Support is glorified in the world of Brahman.

This sacred Word is the highest symbol of the Absolute. He who through meditating on It grasps Its full significance, realizes the glory of God and at once has all his desires satisfied, because God is the fulfilment of all desires.

~ XVIII ~

This Self is never born, nor does It die. It did not spring from anything, nor did anything spring from It. This Ancient One is unborn, eternal, everlasting. It is not slain even though the body is slain.

~ XIX ~

If the slayer thinks that he slays, or if the slain thinks that he is slain, both of these know not. For It neither slays nor is It slain.

~ XX ~

The Self is subtler than the subtle, greater than the great; It dwells in the heart of each living being. He who is free from desire and free from grief, with mind and senses tranquil, beholds the glory of the Atman.

Although this Atman dwells in the heart of every living being, yet It is not perceived by ordinary mortals because of Its subtlety. It cannot be perceived by the senses; a finer spiritual sight is required. The heart must be pure and freed from every unworthy selfish desire; the thought must be indrawn from all external objects; mind and body must be under control; when the whole being thus becomes calm and serene, then it is possible to perceive that effulgent Atman. It is subtler than the subtle, because It is the invisible essence of every thing; and It is greater than the great because It is the boundless, sustaining power of the whole universe; that upon which all existence rests.

∽ XXI ∽

Though sitting, It travels far; though lying, It goes everywhere. Who else save me is fit to know that God, who is (both) joyful and joyless?

The Self is all-pervading, hence It is that which sits still and that which travels, that which is active and that which is inactive.

It is both stationary and moving, and It is the basis of all forms of existence; therefore whatever exists in the universe, whether joy or joylessness, pleasure or pain, must spring from It. Who is better able to know God than I myself, since He resides in my heart and is the very essence of my being? Such should be the attitude of one who is seeking.

~ XXII ~

The wise who know the Self, bodiless, seated within perishable bodies, great and all-pervading, grieve not.

Then a wise man through the practice of discrimination has seen clearly the distinction between body and Soul, he knows that his true Self is not the body, though It dwells in the body. Thus realizing the indestructible, all-pervading nature of his real Self, he surmounts all fear of death or loss, and is not moved even by the greatest sorrow.

∽ XXIII ∽

This Self cannot be attained by study of the Scriptures, nor by intellectual perception, nor by frequent hearing (of It); He whom the Self chooses, by him alone is It attained. To him the Self reveals Its true nature.

We may imagine that by much study we can find out God; but merely hearing about a thing and gaining an intellectual comprehension of it does not mean attaining true knowledge of it. Knowledge only comes through direct perception, and direct perception of God is possible for those alone who are pure in heart and spiritually awakened. Although He is alike to all beings and His mercy is on all, yet the impure and worldy-minded do not get the blessing, because they do not know how to open their hearts to it. He who longs for God, him the Lord chooses; because to him alone can He reveal His true nature.

∽ XXIV ∽

He who has not turned away from evil conduct, whose senses are uncontrolled, who is not tranquil, whose mind is not at rest, he can never attain this Atman even by knowledge.

Yama having first described what the Atman is, now tells us how to attain It. man must try to subdue his lower nature and gain control over the body and senses. e must conquer the impure selfish desires which now disturb the serenity of his mind, that it may grow calm and peaceful. In other words, he must live the life and develop all spiritual qualities in order to perceive the Atman.

~ XXV ~

Who then can know where is this mighty Self? He (that Self) to whom the Brahmanas and Kshatriyas are but food and death itself a condiment.

This text proclaims the glory and majesty of the Supreme. The Brahmanas stand for spiritual strength, the Kshatriyas for physical strength, yet both are overpowered by His mightiness. Life and death alike are food for Him. As the light of the great sun swallows up all the lesser lights of the universe, similarly all worlds are lost in the effulgence of the Eternal Omnipresent Being.

KATHA-UPANISHAD

PART THIRD

~ I ~

There are two who enjoy the fruits of their good deeds in the world, having entered into the cave of the heart, seated (there) on the highest summit. The knowers of Brahman call them shadow and light. So also (they are called) by householders who perform five fire- sacrifices or three Nachiketa fire-sacrifices.

Here the two signify the Higher Self and the lower self, dwelling in the innermost cave of the heart. The Seers of Truth, as well as householders who follow the path of rituals and outer forms with the hope of enjoying the fruits of their good deeds, both proclaim that the Higher Self is like a light and the lower self like a shadow. When the Truth shines clearly in the heart of the knower, then he surmounts the apparent duality of his nature and becomes convinced that there is but One, and that all outer manifestations are nothing but reflections or projections of that One.

II

May we be able to learn that Nachiketa fire-sacrifice, which is a bridge for those who perform sacrifice. May we also know the One, who is the highest imperishable Brahman for those who desire to cross over to the other shore which is beyond fear.

The significance of this text is May we acquire the knowledge of Brahman, the Supreme, in both manifested and unmanifested form. He is manifested as the Lord of sacrifice for those who follow the path of ritual He is the unmanifested, eternal, universal Supreme Being for those who follow the path of wisdom. The "other shore," being the realm of immortality, is said to be beyond fear; because disease, death, and all that which mortals fear, cease to exist there. It is believed by many that these two opening verses were a later interpolation.

III

Know the Atman (Self) as the lord of the chariot, and the body as the chariot. Know also the intellect to be the driver and mind the reins.

IV

The senses are called the horses; the sense objects are the roads; when the Atman is united with body, senses and mind, then the wise call Him the enjoyer.

In the third chapter Yama defines what part of our being dies and what part is deathless, what is mortal and what is immortal. But the Atman, the Higher Self, is so entirely beyond human conception that it is impossible to give a direct definition of It. Only through similies can some idea of It be conveyed. That is the reason why all the great Teachers of the world have so often taught in the form of parables. So here the Ruler of Death represents the Self as the lord of this chariot of the body. The intellect or discriminative faculty is the driver, who controls these wild horses of the senses by holding firmly the reins of the mind. The roads over which these horses travel are made up of all the external objects which attract or repel the senses:—the sense of smelling follows the path of sweet odours, the sense of seeing the way of beautiful sights. Thus each sense, unless restrained by the discriminative faculty, seeks to go out towards its special objects. When the Self is joined with body, mind and senses, It is called the intelligent enjoyer; because It is the one who wills, feels, perceives and does everything.

∾ V ∾

He who is without discrimination and whose mind is always uncontrolled, his senses are unmanageable, like the vicious horses of a driver.

∾ VI ∾

But he who is full of discrimination and whose mind is always controlled, his senses are manageable, like the good horses of a driver.

The man whose intellect is not discriminative and who fails to distinguish right from wrong, the real from the unreal, is carried away by his sense passions and desires, just as a driver is carried away by vicious horses over which he has lost control. But he who clearly distinguishes what is good from what is merely pleasant, and controls all his out-going forces from running after apparent momentary pleasures, his senses obey and serve him as good horses obey their driver.

~ VII ~

He who does not possess discrimination, whose mind is uncontrolled and always impure, he does not reach that goal, but falls again into Samsara (realm of birth and death).

VIII

But he who possesses right discrimination, whose mind is under control and always pure, he reaches that goal, from which he is not born again.

IX

The man who has a discriminative intellect for the driver, and a controlled mind for the reins, reaches the end of the journey, the highest place of Vishnu (the All-pervading and Unchangeable One).

A driver must possess first a thorough knowledge of the road; next he must understand how to handle the reins and control his horses. Then will he drive safely to his destination. Similarly in this journey of life, our mind and senses must be wholly under the control of our higher discriminative faculty; for only when all our forces work in unison can we hope to reach the goal—the abode of Absolute Truth.

◈ X ◈

Beyond the senses are the objects, beyond the objects is the mind, beyond the mind is the intellect, beyond the intellect is the great Atman.

XI

Beyond the great Atman is the Unmanifested; beyond the Unmanifested is the Purusha (the Cosmic Soul); beyond the Purusha there is nothing. That is the end, that is the final goal.

In these two verses the Teacher shows the process of discrimination, by which one attains knowledge of the subtle Self. Beginning with the sense-organs, he leads up to the less and less gross, until he reaches that which is subtlest of all, the true Self of man. The senses are dependent on sense-objects, because without these the senses would have no utility. Superior to sense-objects is the mind, because unless these objects affect the mind, they cannot influence the senses. Over the mind the determinative faculty exercises power; this determinative faculty is governed by the individual Self; beyond this Self is the undifferentiated creative energy known as Avyaktam; and above this is the Purusha or

Supreme Self. Than this there is nothing higher. That is the goal, the Highest Abode of Peace and Bliss.

~ XII ~

This Atman (Self), hidden in all beings, does not shine forth; but It is seen by subtle seers through keen and subtle understanding.

If It dwells in all living beings, why do we not see It? Because the ordinary man's vision is too dull and distracted. It is visible to those alone whose intellect has been purified by constant thought on the Supreme, and whose sight therefore has become refined and sharpened. This keenness of vision comes only when all our forces have been made one-pointed through steadfast practice of concentration and meditation.

~ XIII ~

A wise man should control speech by mind, mind by intellect, intellect by the great Atman, and that by the Peaceful One (the Paramatman or Supreme Self).

Here Yama gives the practical method to be followed if one wishes to realize the Supreme. The word "speech" stands for all the senses. First, therefore, a man must control his outgoing senses by the mind. Then the mind must be brought under the control of the discriminative faculty; that is, it must be withdrawn from all sense-objects and cease to waste its energies on nonessential things. The discriminative faculty in turn must be controlled by the higher individual intelligence and this must be governed wholly by the Supreme Intelligence.

XIV

Arise! Awake! Having reached the Great Ones (illumined Teachers), gain understanding. The path is as sharp as a razor, impassable and difficult to travel, so the wise declare.

This is the eternal call of the wise: Awake from the slumber of ignorance! Arise and seek out those who know the Truth, because only those who have direct vision of Truth are capable of teaching It. Invoke their blessing with a humble spirit and seek to be instructed by them. The path is very difficult to tread. No thoughtless or lethargic person can safely travel on it. One must be strong, wakeful and persevering.

XV

Knowing That which is soundless, touchless, formless, undecaying; also tasteless, odorless, and eternal; beginningless, endless and immutable; beyond the Unmanifested: (knowing That) man escapes from the mouth of death.

The Ruler of Death defines here the innermost essence of our being. Because of its extreme subtlety, it cannot be heard or felt or smelled or tasted like any ordinary object. It never dies. It has no beginning or end. It is unchangeable. Realizing this Supreme Reality, man escapes from death and attains everlasting life. Thus the Teacher has gradually led Nachiketas to a point where he can reveal to him the secret of death. The boy had thought that there was a place where he could stay and become immortal. But Yama shows him that immortality is a state of consciousness and is not gained so long as man clings to name and form, or to perishable objects. What dies? Form. Therefore the formful man dies; but not that which dwells within. Although inconceivably subtle, the Sages have always made an effort through similies and analogies to give some idea of this inner Self or the God within. They have described It as beyond mind and speech; too subtle for ordinary perception, but not beyond the range of purified vision.

XVI

The intelligent man, who has heard and repeated the ancient story of Nachiketas, told by the Ruler of Death, is glorified in the world of Brahman.

XVII

He who with devotion recites this highest secret of immortality before an assembly of Brahmanas (pious men) or at the time of Shraddha (funeral ceremonies), gains everlasting reward, he gains everlasting reward.

PART FOURTH

~ I ~

The Self-existent created the senses outgoing; for this reason man sees the external, but not the inner Atman (Self). Some wise man, however, desiring immortality, with eyes turned away (from the external) sees the Atman within.

In the last chapter the Ruler of Death instructed Nachiketas regarding the nature and glory of the Self. Now he shows the reason why the Self is not seen by the majority. It is because man's mind is constantly drawn outward through the channels of his senses, and this prevents his seeing the inner Self (Pratyagatman); but now and then a seeker, wiser than others, goes within and attains the vision of the undying Self.

II

Children (the ignorant) pursue external pleasures; (thus) they fall into the wide-spread snare of death. But the wise, knowing the nature of immortality, do not seek the permanent among fleeting things.

Those who are devoid of discrimination and fail to distinguish between real and unreal, the fleeting and the permanent, set their hearts on the changeable things of this world; hence they entangle themselves in the net of insatiable desire, which leads inevitably to disappointment and suffering. To such, death must seem a reality because they identify themselves with that which is born and which dies. But the wise, who see deeper into the nature of things, are no longer deluded by the charm of the phenomenal world and do not seek for permanent happiness among its passing enjoyments.

III

That by which one knows form, taste, smell, sound, touch and sense enjoyments, by That also one knows whatever remains (to be known). This verily is That (which thou hast asked to know).

IV

That by which a mortal perceives, both in dream and in waking, by knowing that great all-pervading Atman the wise man grieves no more.

In these verses the teacher tries to make plain that all knowledge, as well as all sense perception, in every state of consciousness—sleeping, dreaming or waking—is possible only because the Self exists. There can be no knowledge or perception independent of the Self. Wise men, aware of this, identify themselves with their Higher Self and thus transcend the realm of grief.

V

He who knows this Atman, the honey-eater (perceiver and enjoyer of objects), ever near, as the lord of the past and future, fears no more. This verily is That.

VI

He who sees Him seated in the five elements, born of Tapas (fire of Brahman), born before water; who, having entered the cave of the heart, abides therein —this verily is That.

This verse indicates that He, the Great Self, is the cause of all created objects. According to the Vedas, His first manifestation was Brahma, the Personal God or Creator, born of the fire of wisdom. He existed before the evolution of the five elements— earth, water, fire, air and ether; hence He was "born before water." He is the Self dwelling in the hearts of all creatures.

VII

He who knows Aditi, who rises with Prana (the Life Principle), existent in all the Devas; who, having entered into the heart, abides there; and who was born from the elements— this verily is That.

This verse is somewhat obscure and

seems like an interpolated amplification of the preceding verse.

∽ VIII ∾

Tje all-seeing fire which exists hidden in the two sticks, as the foetus is well-guarded in the womb by the mother, (that fire) is to be worshipped day after day by wakeful seekers (after wisdom), as well as by sacrificers. This verily is That.

Fire is called all-seeing because its light makes everything visible. In Vedic sacrifices the altar fire was always kindled by rubbing together two sticks of a special kind of wood called Arani. Because fire was regarded as one of the most perfect symbols of Divine wisdom, it was to be worshipped by all seekers after Truth, whether they followed the path of meditation or the path of rituals.

IX

From whence the sun rises, and whither it goes at setting, upon That all the Devas depend. No one goes beyond That. This verily is That.

X

What is here (in the visible world), that is there (in the invisible); he who sees difference (between visible and invisible) goes from death to death.

XI

By mind alone this is to be realized. There is no difference whatever (between visible and invisible). He who sees difference here (between these) goes from death to death.

In the sight of true wisdom, there is no difference between the creator and the created. Even physical science has come to recognize that cause and effect are but two aspects of one manifestation of energy. He who fails to see this, being engrossed in the visible only, goes from death to death; because he clings to external forms which are perishable. Only the essence which dwells within is unchangeable and imperishable. This knowledge of the oneness of visible and invisible, however, cannot be acquired through sense-perception. It can only be attained by the purified mind.

XII

The Purusha (Self), of the size of a thumb, resides in the middle of the body as the lord of the past and the future, (he who knows Him) fears no more. This verily is That.

The seat of the Purusha is said to be the heart, hence It "resides in the middle of the body." Although It is limitless and all-pervading, yet in relation to Its abiding-place It is represented as limited in extension, "the size of a thumb." This refers really to the heart, which in shape may be likened to a thumb. s light is everywhere, yet we see it focused in a lamp and believe it to be there only; similarly, although the life-current flows everywhere in the body, the heart is regarded as peculiarly its seat.

XIII

That Purusha, of the size of a thumb, is like a light without smoke, lord of the past and the future. He is the same today and tomorrow. This verily is That.

In this verse the teacher defines the effulgent nature of the Soul, whose light is pure like a flame without smoke. He also answers the question put by Nachiketas as to what happens after death, by declaring that no real change takes place, because the Soul is ever the same.

XIV

As rain water, (falling) on the mountain top, runs down over the rocks on all sides; similarly, he who sees difference (between visible forms) runs after them in various directions.

~ XV ~

O Gautama (Nachiketas), as pure water poured into pure water becomes one, so also is it with the Self of an illumined Knower (he becomes one with the Supreme).

KATHA-UPANISHAD

PART FIFTH

I

The city of the Unborn, whose knowledge is unchanging, has eleven gates. Thinking on Him, man grieves no more; and being freed (from ignorance), he attains liberation. This verily is That.

This human body is called a city with eleven gates, where the eternal unborn Spirit dwells. These gates are the two eyes, two ears, two nostrils, the mouth, the navel, the two lower apertures, and the imperceptible opening at the top of the head. The Self or Atman holds the position of ruler in this city; and being above the modifications of birth, death and all human imperfections, It is not affected by the changes of the physical organism. As the intelligent man through constant thought and meditation realizes the splendour of this Supreme Spirit, he becomes free from that part of his nature which grieves and suffers, and thus he attains liberation.

~ II ~

He is the sun dwelling in the bright heaven; He is the air dwelling in space; He is the fire burning on the altar; He is the guest dwelling in the house. He dwells in man. He dwells in those greater than man. He dwells in sacrifice. He dwells in the ether. He is (all that is) born in water, (all that) is born in earth, (all that) is born in sacrifice, (all that) is born on mountains. He is the True and the Great.

~ III ~

He it is who sends the (in-coming) Prana (life-breath) upward and throws the (out-going) breath downward. Him all the senses worship, the adorable Atman, seated in the centre (the heart).

~ IV ~

When this Atman, which is seated in the body, goes out (from the body), what remains then? This verily is That.

V

No mortal lives by the in-coming breath (Prana) or by the out-going breath (Apana), but he lives by another on which these two depend.

VI

O Gautama (Nachiketas), I shall declare unto thee the secret of the eternal Brahman and what happens to the Self after death.

VII

Some Jivas (individual Souls) enter wombs to be embodied; others go into immovable forms, according to their deeds and knowledge.

This text shows the application of the law of cause and effect to all forms of life. The thoughts and actions of the present life determine the future birth and environment.

VIII

The Being who remains awake while all sleep, who grants all desires, That is pure, That is Brahman, That alone is said to be immortal. On That all the worlds rest. None goes beyond That. This verily is That.

~ IX ~

As fire, though one, having entered the world, becomes various according to what it burns, so does the Atman (Self) within all living beings, though one, become various according to what it enters. It also exists outside.

~ X ~

As air, though one, having entered the world, becomes various according to what it enters, so does the Atman within all living beings, though one, become various according to what it enters. It also exists outside.

By using these similies of fire and air, the teacher tries to show Nachiketas the subtle quality of the great Self, who, although one and formless like air and fire, yet assumes different shapes according to the form in which It dwells. But, being all-pervading and unlimited, It cannot be confined to these forms; therefore it is said that It also exists outside all forms.

∽ XI ∽

As the sun, the eye of the whole world, is not defiled by external impurities seen by the eyes, thus the one inner Self of all living beings is not defiled by the misery of the world, being outside it.

The sun is called the eye of the world because it reveals all objects. As the sun may shine on the most impure object, yet remain uncontaminated by it, so the Divine Self within is not touched by the impurity or suffering of the physical form in which it dwells, the Self being beyond all bodily limitations.

~ XII ~

There is one ruler, the Self of all living beings, who makes the one form manifold; the wise who perceive Him seated within their Self, to them belongs eternal bliss, not to others.

~ XIII ~

Eternal among the changing, consciousness of the conscious, who, though one, fulfils the desires of many: the wise who perceive Him seated within their Self, to them belongs eternal peace, not to others.

XIV

They (the wise) perceive that indescribable highest bliss, saying, This is That. How am I to know It? Does It shine (by Its own light) or does It shine (by reflected light)?

XV

The sun does not shine there, nor the moon, nor the stars; nor do these lightnings shine there, much less this fire. When He shines, everything shines after Him; by His light all is lighted.

PART SIXTH

~ I ~

This ancient Aswattha tree has its root above and branches below. That is pure, That is Brahman, That alone is called the Immortal. All the worlds rest in That. None goes beyond That. This verily is That.

This verse indicates the origin of the tree of creation (the Samsara-Vriksha), which is rooted above in Brahman, the Supreme, and sends its branches downward into the phenomenal world. Heat and cold, pleasure and pain, birth and death, and all the shifting conditions of the mortal realm—these are the branches; but the origin of the tree, the Brahman, is eternally pure, unchanging, free and deathless. From the highest angelic form to the minutest atom, all created things have their origin in Him. He is the foundation of the universe. There is nothing beyond Him.

II

Whatever there is in the universe is evolved from Prana and vibrates in Prana. That is a mighty terror, like an upraised thunderbolt. They who know That become immortal.

III

From fear of Him the fire burns, from fear of Him the sun shines. From fear of Him Indra and Vayu and Death, the fifth, speed forth.

Just as the body cannot live or act without the Soul, similarly nothing in the created world can exist independent of Brahman, who is the basis of all existence. His position is like that of a king whom all must obey; hence it is said that the gods of sun, moon, wind, rain, do His bidding. He is likened to an upraised thunderbolt, because of the impartial and inevitable nature of His law, which all powers, great or small, must obey absolutely.

IV

If a man is not able to know Him before the dissolution of the body, then he becomes embodied again in the created worlds.

As soon as a man acquires knowledge of the Supreme, he is liberated; but if he fails to attain such knowledge before his Soul is separated from the body, then he must take other bodies and return again and again to this realm of birth and death, until through varied experience he realizes the nature of the Supreme and his relation to Him.

V

As in a mirror, so is He seen within oneself; as in a dream, so (is He seen) in the world of the fathers (departed spirits); as in water, so (is He seen) in the world of Gandharvas (the angelic realm). As light and shadow, so (is He seen) in the world of Brahma (the Creator).

When by means of a purified understanding one beholds God within, the image is distinct as in a polished mirror; but one cannot have clear vision of the Supreme by attaining to the various realms known as heavens, where one reaps the fruit of his good deeds. It is only by developing one's highest consciousness here in this life that perfect God-vision can be attained.

VI

Knowing that the senses are distinct (from the Atman) and their rising and setting separate (from the Atman), a wise man grieves no more.

A wise man never confounds the Atman, which is birthless and deathless, with that which has beginning and end. Therefore, when he sees his senses and his physical organism waxing and waning, he knows that his real Self within can never be affected by these outer changes, so he remains unmoved.

VII

Higher than the senses is the mind, higher than the mind is the intellect, higher than the intellect is the great Atman, higher than the Atman is the Unmanifested.

VIII

Beyond the Unmanifested is the all-pervading and imperceptible Being (Purusha). By knowing Him, the mortal is liberated and attains immortality.

This division of the individual into senses, mind, intellect, self-consciousness, undifferentiated creative energy and the Absolute Self is explained in the commentary of verse XI, Part Third.

IX

His form is not to be seen. No one can see Him with the eye. He is perceived by the heart, by the intellect and by the mind. They who know this become immortal.

The Supreme, being formless, cannot be discerned by the senses, hence all knowledge of Him must be acquired by the subtler faculties of heart, intellect and mind, which are developed only through the purifying practice of meditation.

∽ X ∾

When the five organs of perception become still, together with the mind, and the intellect ceases to be active: that is called the highest state.

The teacher now shows Nachiketas the process by which the transcendental vision can be attained. he out-going senses,—seeing, hearing, smelling, touching, tasting; the restless mind and the intellect: all must be indrawn and quieted. The state of equilibrium thus attained is called the highest state, because all the forces of one's being become united and focused; and this inevitably leads to supersensuous vision.

~ XI ~

This firm holding back of the senses is what is known as Yoga. Then one should become watchful, for Yoga comes and goes.

Yoga literally means to join or to unite the lower self with the Higher Self, the object with the subject, the worshipper with God. In order to gain this union, however, one must first disunite oneself from all that scatters the physical, mental and intellectual forces; so the outgoing perceptions must be detached from the external world and indrawn. When this is accomplished through constant practice of concentration and meditation, the union takes place of its own accord. But it may be lost again, unless one is watchful.

XII

He cannot be attained by speech, by mind, or by the eye. How can That be realized except by him who says "He is"?

XIII

He should be realized as "He is" and also as the reality of both (visible and invisible). He who knows Him as "He is," to him alone His real nature is revealed.

This supersensuous vision cannot be gained through man's ordinary faculties. By mind, eye, or speech the manifested attributes of the Divine can be apprehended; but only one who has acquired the supersensuous sight can directly perceive God's existence and declare definitely that "He is," that He alone exists in both the visible and the invisible world.

~ XIV ~

When all desires dwelling in the heart cease, then the mortal becomes immortal and attains Brahman here.

~ XV ~

When all the ties of the heart are cut asunder here, then the mortal becomes immortal. Such is the teaching.

XVI

There are a hundred and one nerves of the heart. One of them penetrates the centre of the head. Going upward through it, one attains immortality. The other (hundred nerve-courses) lead, in departing, to different worlds.

The nervous system of the body provides the channels through which the mind travels; the direction in which it moves is determined by its desires and tendencies. When the mind becomes pure and desireless, it takes the upward course and at the time of departing passes out through the imperceptible opening at the crown of the head; but as long as it remains full of desires, its course is downward towards the realms where those desires can be satisfied.

XVII

The Purusha, the inner Self, of the size of a thumb, is ever seated in the heart of all living beings. With perseverance man should draw Him out from his body as one draws the inner stalk from a blade of grass. One should know Him as pure and deathless, as pure and deathless.

As has been explained in Part Fourth, verse XII, the inner Self, although unlimited, is described as "the size of a thumb" because of its abiding-place in the heart, often likened to a lotus-bud which is similar to a thumb in size and shape. Through the process of steadfast discrimination, one should learn to differentiate the Soul from the body, just as one separates the pith from a reed.

⚘ XVIII ⚘

Thus Nachiketas, having acquired this wisdom taught by the Ruler of Death, together with all the rules of Yoga, became free from impurity and death and attained Brahman (the Supreme). So also will it be with another who likewise knows the nature of the Self.

PEACE CHANT

May He (the Supreme Being) protect us both. May He be pleased with us. May we acquire strength. May our study bring us illumination. May there be no enmity among us.

OM! PEACE! PEACE! PEACE!

Here ends this Upanishad

KENA-UPANISHAD

KENA-UPANISHAD

Like the Isavasya, this Upanishad derives its name from the opening word of the text, Kena-ishitam, "by whom directed." It is also known as the Talavakara-Upanishad because of its place as a chapter in the Talavakara-Brahmana of the Sama-Veda.

Among the Upanishads it is one of the most analytical and metaphysical, its purpose being to lead the mind from the gross to the subtle, from effect to cause. By a series of profound questions and answers, it seeks to locate the source of man's being; and to expand his self-consciousness until it has become identical with God-Consciousness.

KENA-UPANISHAD

Peace Chant

May my limbs, speech, Prana (life-force), sight, hearing, strength and all my senses, gain in vigor. All is the Brahman (Supreme Lord) of the Upanishads. May I never deny the Brahman. May the Brahman never deny me. May there be no denial of the Brahman. May there be no separation from the Brahman. May all the virtues declared in the sacred Upanishads be manifest in me, who am devoted to the Atman (Higher Self). May they be manifest in me.

OM! PEACE! PEACE! PEACE!

KENA-UPANISHAD

PART FIRST

~ I ~

By whom commanded and directed does the mind go towards its objects? Commanded by whom does the life-force, the first (cause), move? At whose will do men utter speech? What power directs the eye and the ear?

Thus the disciple approached the Master and inquired concerning the cause of life and human activity. Having a sincere longing for Truth he desired to know who really sees and hears, who actuates the apparent physical man. He perceived all about him the phenomenal world, the existence of which he could prove by his senses; but he sought to know the invisible causal world, of which he was now only vaguely conscious. Is mind all-pervading and all-powerful, or is it impelled by some other force, he asked. Who sends forth the vital energy, without which nothing can exist? The teacher replies:

II

It is the ear of the ear, the mind of the mind, the speech of the speech, the life of the life, the eye of the eye. The wise, freed (from the senses and from mortal desires), after leaving this world, become immortal.

An ordinary man hears, sees, thinks, but he is satisfied to know only as much as can be known through the senses; he does not analyze and try to find that which stands behind the ear or eye or mind. He is completely identified with his external nature. His conception does not go beyond the little circle of his bodily life, which concerns the outer man only. He has no consciousness of that which enables his senses and organs to perform their tasks.

There is a vast difference between the manifested form and That which is manifested through the form. When we know That, we shall not die with the body. One who clings to the senses and to things that are ephemeral, must die many deaths, but that man who knows the eye of the eye, the ear of the ear, having severed himself from his physical nature, becomes immortal. Immortality is attained when man transcends his apparent nature and finds that subtle, eternal and inexhaustible essence which is within him.

∽ III ∽

There the eye does not go, nor speech, nor mind. We do not know That; we do not understand how It can be taught. It is distinct from the known and also It is beyond the unknown. Thus we have heard from the ancient (teachers) who told us about It.

These physical eyes are unable to perceive that subtle essence. Nor can it be expressed by finite language or known by finite intelligence, because it is infinite. Our conception of knowing finite things is to know their name and form; but knowledge of God must be distinct from such knowledge. This is why some declare God to be unknown and unknowable; because He is far more than eye or mind or speech can perceive, comprehend or express. The Upanishad does not say that He cannot be known. He is unknowable to man's finite nature. How can a finite mortal apprehend the Infinite Whole? But He can be known by man's God-like nature.

IV

That which speech does not illumine, but which illumines speech: know that alone to be the Brahman (the Supreme Being), not this which people worship here.

V

That which cannot be thought by mind, but by which, they say, mind is able to think: know that alone to be the Brahman, not this which people worship here.

VI

That which is not seen by the eye, but by which the eye is able to see: know that alone to be the Brahman, not this which people worship here.

VII

That which cannot be heard by the ear, but by which the ear is able to hear: know that alone to be Brahman, not this which people worship here.

VIII

That which none breathes with the breath, but by which breath is in-breathed: know that alone to be the Brahman, not this which people worship here.

Ordinarily we know three states of consciousness only,—waking, dreaming and sleeping. There is, however, a fourth state, the superconscious, which transcends these. In the first three states the mind is not clear enough to save us from error; but in the fourth state it gains such purity of vision that it can perceive the Divine. If God could be known by the limited mind and senses, then God-knowledge would be like any other knowledge and spiritual science like any physical science. He can be known, however, by the purified mind only. Therefore to know God, man must purify himself. The mind described in the Upanishads is the superconscious mind. According to the Vedic Sages the mind in its ordinary state is only another sense organ. This mind is limited, but when it becomes illumined by the light of the Cosmic Intelligence, or the "mind of the mind," then it is able to apprehend the First Cause or That which stands behind all external activities.

PART SECOND

I

If thou thinkest "I know It well," then it is certain that thou knowest but little of the Brahman (Absolute Truth), or in what form He (resideth) in the Devas (minor aspects of Deity). Therefore I think that what thou thinkest to be known is still to be sought after.

Having given the definition of the real Self or Brahman, by which mortals are able to see, hear, feel and think, the teacher was afraid that the disciple, after merely hearing about It, might conclude that he knew It. So he said to him: "You have heard about It, but that is not enough. You must experience It. Mere intellectual recognition will not give you true knowledge of It. Neither can It be taught to you. The teacher can only show the way. You must find It for yourself."

Knowledge means union between

subject and object. To gain this union one must practice, theory cannot help us. The previous chapter has shown that the knowledge of Brahman is beyond sense-perception: "There the eye does not go, nor speech, nor mind." "That is distinct from known and also It is beyond the unknown." Therefore it was necessary for the teacher to remind the disciple that knowledge based on sense-perception or intellectual apprehension should not be confounded with supersensuous knowledge. Although the disciple had listened to the teacher with unquestioning mind and was intellectually convinced of the truth of his words, it was now necessary for him to prove by his own experience what he had heard. Guided by the teacher, he sought within himself through meditation the meaning of Brahman; and having gained a new vision, he approached the teacher once more.

II

The disciple said: I do not think I know It well, nor do I think that I do not know It. He among us who knows It truly, knows (what is meant by) "I know" and also what is meant by "I know It not."

This appears to be contradictory, but it is not. In the previous chapter we learned that Brahman is "distinct from the known" and "beyond the unknown." The disciple, realizing this, says: "So far as mortal conception is concerned, I do not think I know, because I understand that It is beyond mind and speech; yet from the higher point of view, I cannot say that I do not know; for the very fact that I exist, that I can seek It, shows that I know; for It is the source of my being. I do not know, however, in the sense of knowing the whole Infinite Ocean of existence." The word knowledge is used ordinarily to signify acquaintance with phenomena only, but man must transcend this relative knowledge before he can have a clear conception of God. One who wishes to attain Soul-consciousness must rise above matter.

The observation of material science being confined to the sense plane, it ignores what is beyond. Therefore it must always be limited and subject to change. It discovered atoms, then it went further and discovered electrons, and when it had found the one, it had to drop the other; so this kind of knowledge can never lead to the ultimate knowledge of the Infinite, because it is exclusive and not inclusive. Spiritual science is not merely a question of mind and brain, it depends on the awakening of our latent higher consciousness.

~ III ~

He who thinks he knows It not, knows It. He who thinks he knows It, knows It not. The true knowers think they can never know It (because of Its infinitude), while the ignorant think they know It.

By this text the teacher confirms the idea that Brahman is unthinkable, because unconditioned. Therefore he says: He who considers It beyond thought, beyond sense-perception, beyond mind and speech, he alone has a true understanding of Brahman. They who judge a living being from his external form and sense faculties, know him not; because the real Self of man is not manifested in his seeing, hearing, speaking. His real Self is that within by which he hears and speaks and sees. In the same way he knows not Brahman who thinks he knows It by name and form. The arrogant and foolish man thinks he knows everything; but the true knower is humble. He says: "How can I know Thee, who art Infinite and beyond mind and speech?" In the last portion of the text, the teacher draws an impressive contrast between the attitude of the wise man who knows, but thinks he does not know; and that of the ignorant who does not know, but thinks he knows.

IV

It (Brahman) is known, when It is known in every state of consciousness. (Through such knowledge) one attains immortality. By attaining this Self, man gains strength; and by Self-knowledge immortality is attained.

We have learned from the previous text that the Brahman is unknown to those whose knowledge is limited to sense experience; but He is not unknown to those whose purified intelligence perceives Him as the basis of all states of consciousness and the essence of all things. By this higher knowledge a man attains immortality, because he knows that although his body may decay and die, the subtle essence of his being remains untouched. Such an one also acquires unlimited strength, because he identifies himself with the ultimate Source. The strength which comes from one's own muscle and brain or from one's individual power must be limited and mortal and therefore cannot lift one beyond death; but through the strength which Atma-gnana or Self-knowledge gives, immortality is reached. Whenever knowledge is based on direct perception of this undying essence, one transcends all fear of death and becomes immortal.

V

If one knows It here, that is Truth; if one knows It not here, then great is his loss. The wise seeing the same Self in all beings, being liberated from this world, become immortal.

PART THIRD

I

The Brahman once won a victory for the Devas. Through that victory of the Brahman, the Devas became elated. They thought, "This victory is ours. This glory is ours."

Brahman here does not mean a personal Deity. There is a Brahma, the first person of the Hindu Trinity; but Brahman is the Absolute, the One without a second, the essence of all. There are different names and forms which represent certain personal aspects of Divinity, such as Brahma the Creator, Vishnu the Preserver and Siva the Transformer; but no one of these can fully represent the Whole. Brahman is the vast ocean of being, on which rise numberless ripples and waves of manifestation. From the smallest atomic form to a Deva or an angel, all spring from that limitless ocean of Brahman, the inexhaustible

Source of life. No manifested form of life can be independent of its source, just as no wave, however mighty, can be independent of the ocean. Nothing moves without that Power. He is the only Doer. But the Devas thought: "This victory is ours, this glory is ours."

~ II ~

The Brahman perceived this and appeared before them. They did not know what mysterious form it was.

III

They said to Fire: "O Jataveda (All-knowing)! Find out what mysterious spirit this is." He said: "Yes."

IV

He ran towards it and He (Brahman) said to him: "Who art thou?" "I am Agni, I am Jataveda," he (the Fire-god) replied.

V

Brahman asked: "What power resides in thee?" Agni replied: "I can burn up all whatsoever exists on earth."

VI

Brahman placed a straw before him and said: "Burn this." He (Agni) rushed towards it with all speed, but was not able to burn it. So he returned from there and said (to the Devas): "I was not able to find out what this great mystery is."

VII

Then they said to Vayu (the Air-god): "Vayu! Find out what this mystery is." He said: "Yes."

VIII

He ran towards it and He (Brahman) said to him: "Who art thou?" "I am Vayu, I am Matarisva (traveller of Heaven)," he (Vayu) said.

IX

Then the Brahman said: "What power is in thee?" Vayu replied: "I can blow away all whatsoever exists on earth."

X

Brahman placed a straw before him and said: "Blow this away." He (Vayu) rushed towards it with all speed, but was not able to blow it away. So he returned from there and said (to the Devas): "I was not able to find out what this great mystery is."

XI

Then they said to Indra: "O Maghavan (Worshipful One)! Find out what this mystery is." He said: "Yes"; and ran towards it, but it disappeared before him.

⚬ XII ⚬

Then he saw in that very space a woman beautifully adorned, Uma of golden hue, daughter of Haimavat (Himalaya). He asked: "What is this great mystery?"

Here we see how the Absolute assumes concrete form to give knowledge of Himself to the earnest seeker. Brahman, the impenetrable mystery, disappeared and in His place appeared a personal form to represent Him. This is a subtle way of showing the difference between the Absolute and the personal aspects of Deity. The Absolute is declared to be unknowable and unthinkable, but He assumes deified personal aspects to make Himself known to His devotees. Thus Uma, daughter of the Himalaya, represents that personal aspect as the offspring of the Infinite Being; while the Himalaya stands as the symbol of the Eternal, Unchangeable One.

PART FOURTH

I

She (Uma) said: "It is Brahman. It is through the victory of Brahman that ye are victorious." Then from her words, he (Indra) knew that it (that mysterious form) was Brahman.

Uma replied to Indra, "It is to Brahman that you owe your victory. It is through His power that you live and act. He is the agent and you are all only instruments in His hands. Therefore your idea that 'This victory is ours, this glory is ours,' is based on ignorance." At once Indra saw their mistake. The Devas, being puffed up with vanity, had thought they themselves had achieved the victory, whereas it was Brahman; for not even a blade of grass can move without His command.

II

Therefore these Devas,—Agni, Vayu and Indra—excel other Devas, because they came nearer to Brahman. It was they who first knew this spirit as Brahman.

III

Therefore Indra excels all other Devas, because he came nearest to Brahman, and because he first (before all others) knew this spirit as Brahman.

Agni, Vayu and Indra were superior to the other Devas because they gained a closer vision; and they were able to do this because they were purer; while Indra stands as the head of the Devas, because he realized the Truth directly, he reached Brahman. The significance of this is that whoever comes in direct touch with Brahman or the Supreme is glorified.

IV

Thus the teaching of Brahman is here illustrated in regard to the Devas. He dashed like lightning, and appeared and disappeared just as the eye winks.

The teaching as regards the Devas was that Brahman is the only Doer. He had appeared before them in a mysterious form; but the whole of the unfathomable Brahman could not be seen in any definite form; so at the moment of vanishing, He manifested more of His immeasurable glory and fleetness of action by a sudden dazzling flash of light.

V

Next (the teaching) is regarding Adhyatman (the embodied Soul). The mind seems to approach Him (Brahman). By this mind (the seeker) again and again remembers and thinks about Brahman.

Only by the mind can the seeker after knowledge approach Brahman, whose nature in glory and speed has been described as like unto a flash of lightning. Mind alone can picture the indescribable Brahman; and mind alone, being swift in its nature, can follow Him. It is through the help of this mind that we can think and meditate on Brahman; and when by constant thought of Him the mind becomes purified, then like a polished mirror it can reflect His Divine Glory.

VI

That Brahman is called Tadvanam (object of adoration). He is to be worshipped by the name Tadvanam. He who knows Brahman thus, is loved by all beings.

Brahman is the object of adoration and the goal of all beings. For this reason he should be worshipped and meditated upon as Tadvanam. Whoever knows Him in this aspect becomes one with Him, and serves as a clear channel through which the blessings of Brahman flow out to others. The knower of God partakes of all His lovable qualities and is therefore loved by all true devotees.

KENA-UPANISHAD

∼ VII ∼

The disciple asked: O Master, teach me the Upanishad. (The teacher replied:) The Upanishad has been taught thee. We have certainly taught thee the Upanishad about Brahman.

∼ VIII ∼

The Upanishad is based on tapas (practice of the control of body, mind and senses), dama (subjugation of the senses), karma (right performance of prescribed actions). The Vedas are its limbs. Truth is its support.

IX

He who knows this (wisdom of the Upanishad), having been cleansed of all sin, becomes established in the blissful, eternal and highest abode of Brahman, in the highest abode of Brahman.

HERE ENDS THIS UPANISHAD

KENA-UPANISHAD

This Upanishad is called Kena, because it begins with the inquiry: "By whom" (Kena) willed or directed does the mind go towards its object? From whom comes life? What enables man to speak, to hear and see? And the teacher in reply gives him the definition of Brahman, the Source and Basis of existence. The spirit of the Upanishads is always to show that no matter where we look or what we see or feel in the visible world, it all proceeds from one Source.

The prevailing note of all Vedic teaching is this: One tremendous Whole becoming the world, and again the world merging in that Whole. It also strives in various ways to define that Source, knowing which all else is known and without which no knowledge can be well established. So here the teacher replies: That which is the eye of the eye, the ear of the ear, that is the inexhaustible river of being which flows on eternally; while bubbles of creation rise on the surface, live for a time, then burst.

The teacher, however, warns the disciple that this eye, ear, mind, can never perceive

It; for It is that which illumines speech and mind, which enables eye and ear and all sense-faculties to perform their tasks. "It is distinct from the known and also It is beyond the unknown." He who thinks he knows It, knows It not; because It is never known by those who believe that It can be grasped by the intellect or by the senses; but It can be known by him who knows It as the basis of all consciousness.

The knower of Truth says, "I know It not," because he realizes the unbounded, infinite nature of the Supreme. "Thou art this (the visible), Thou art That (the invisible), and Thou art all that is beyond," he declares. The ordinary idea of knowledge is that which is based on sense preceptions; but the knowledge of an illumined Sage is not confined to his senses. He has all the knowledge that comes from the senses and all that comes from Spirit.

The special purpose of this Upanishad is to give us the knowledge of the Real, that we may not come under the dominion of the ego by identifying ourselves with our body, mind and senses. Mortals become mortals because they fall under the sway of ego and depend on their own limited physical and mental strength. The lesson of the parable of the Devas and Brahman is that there is no real power, no real doer except God. He is the eye of the eye, the ear of the ear; and eyes, ears, and all our faculties have no power independent of Him. When we thus realize Him as the underlying Reality of our being, we transcend death and become immortal.

OM! PEACE! PEACE! PEACE!